Stepping into Standards Theme Series

Life Cycles

Written by
Kim Cernek

Editor: Sheri Rous
Illustrator: Jenny Campbell
Cover Illustrators: Darcy Tom and Kimberly Schamber
Designer: Moonhee Pak
Cover Designer: Moonhee Pak
Art Director: Tom Cochrane
Project Director: Carolea Williams

Table of Contents

Introduction

Due to the often-changing national, state, and district standards, it is frequently difficult to "squeeze in" fascinating topics for student enrichment on top of meeting required standards and including a balanced program in your classroom curriculum. The *Stepping into Standards Theme Series* incorporates required subjects and skills for second- and third-grade students while engaging them in an exciting and meaningful theme. Students will participate in a variety of language arts experiences to help them with **reading** and **writing** skills. They will also enjoy **standards-based math activities, hands-on science projects,** and **interactive social studies activities**.

The creative lessons in *Life Cycles* provide imaginative, innovative ideas to help you motivate students as they learn about different life cycles in your classroom. The activities will inspire students to explore life cycles as well as provide them with opportunities to enhance their knowledge and meet state standards. The pretest and posttest will help you assess your students' knowledge of the subject matter and skills.

Invite students to explore life cycles as they
- learn about the stages of various plants' and animals' lives
- observe a plant at each stage of its life cycle
- find the main ideas in a story while learning about the life cycle of an insect
- determine ways to help save endangered species
- compare the development of children in the past with children of today
- create topographical maps to determine the best way for farmers to utilize their land and help animals develop

Each resource book in the *Stepping into Standards Theme Series* includes standards information, numerous activities, easy-to-use reproducibles, and a full-color overhead transparency to help you integrate a fun theme into your required curriculum. You will see how easy it can be to incorporate creative activities with academic requirements while students enjoy their exploration of life cycles!

Getting Started

How to Use This Book

This comprehensive resource is filled with all the components you need to introduce, teach, review, and assess students on key skills while still making their learning experience as memorable as possible. The lessons are divided into four main sections: Language Arts, Math, Science, and Social Studies. Follow these simple steps to maximize student learning.

1 Use the **Meeting Standards** chart (pages 6–7) to help you identify the standards featured in each activity and incorporate them into your curriculum.

2 Review **Introducing . . . Life Cycles** (page 8). This page provides numerous facts about the theme of study, literature selections that work well with the theme, key vocabulary words that your students will encounter while studying the theme, and the answers to all the assessments presented throughout the resource. Use this page to obtain background knowledge and ideas to help you make this a theme to remember!

3 Use the **Life Cycles Pretest** (page 9) to assess your students' prior knowledge of the theme. This short, knowledge-based, multiple-choice test focuses on the key components of life cycles. Use the results to help determine how much introduction to provide for the theme. The test can also be administered again at the end of the unit of study to see how much students have learned.

4 Copy the **What Do You Know? KWL Chart** (page 10) onto an overhead transparency, or enlarge it onto a piece of chart paper. Ask students to share what they already know about life cycles. Record student responses in the "What We **Know**" column. Ask students to share what they would like to know about life cycles. Record student responses in the "What We **Want** to Know" column. Then, set aside the chart. Revisit it at the end of the unit. Ask students to share what they learned about life cycles, and record their responses in the "What We **Learned**" column.

5 Give students the **Life Cycles—Reading Comprehension Test** (pages 11–12). It is a great way to introduce students to the theme while making learning interesting. You can assess your students' comprehension skills as well as introduce students to the components of different life cycles. The multiple-choice questions require students to use literal as well as inferential skills.

6 Use the **Life Cycles full-color transparency** to enhance the theme. Display the transparency at any time during the unit to support the lessons and activities and to help reinforce key concepts about life cycles.

7 Use the activities from the **Language Arts, Math, Science, and Social Studies sections** (pages 13–61) to teach students about life cycles and to help them learn, practice, and review the required standards for their grade level. Each activity includes a list of objectives, a materials list, and a set of easy-to-follow directions. Either complete each section in its entirety before continuing on to the next section, or mix and match activities from each section.

8 Use the skills-based **Life Cycles Cumulative Test** (pages 62–63) to help you assess both what your students learned about the theme and what skills they acquired while studying the theme. It will also help you identify if students are able to apply learned skills to different situations. This cumulative test includes both multiple-choice questions and short-answer questions to provide a well-rounded assessment of your students' knowledge.

9 Upon completion of the unit, reward your students for their accomplishments with the **Certificate of Completion** (page 64). Students are sure to be eager to share their knowledge and certificate with family and friends.

Meeting Standards

Language Arts

	Researching a Life Cycle (PAGE 13)	Dolphin Delivery (PAGE 14)	A Friendly Letter from the Farm (PAGE 15)	Watching the Cycle of Life (PAGE 16)	A Spider Is Born (PAGE 16)	Can You Find the Word? (PAGE 17)	Repeating Rimes in Word Family Words (PAGE 17)	Connecting a Caterpillar (PAGE 18)	Get the Idea? (PAGE 19)	Cycling Together (PAGE 20)	Life Cycle Sounds (PAGE 20)	Growing Up (PAGE 21)
READING												
Alliteration											●	
Comprehension	●	●			●				●	●		●
Rhyming Words							●					
Sequencing									●			●
Story Elements					●				●	●		
Syllabication								●				
Vocabulary Development	●	●	●		●	●	●	●	●		●	
WRITING												
Alphabetical Order								●				
Capitalization		●										
Commas		●										
Editing	●								●			
Friendly Letters			●									
Main Ideas			●	●					●			
Penmanship			●					●	●	●		●
Revision	●											
Sentences				●					●	●		
Spelling						●	●	●				

Meeting Standards

Math
Science
Social Studies

	Life Cycle Math (PAGE 32)	A Time to Grow (PAGE 32)	Measuring My Garden (PAGE 33)	Spiderweb Math (PAGE 33)	Numbers in Nature (PAGE 34)	Life Cycle of a Frog (PAGE 35)	The Carrot Seed (PAGE 42)	Life Cycle Mobiles (PAGE 43)	Life Cycle Circles (PAGE 44)	Life Cycle Memory (PAGE 45)	Baby Basics (PAGE 45)	The Life of a Butterfly (PAGE 46)	Cycles of Life through History (PAGE 54)	Discussions Do Make a Difference (PAGE 55)	Food from the Circle of Life (PAGE 56)	The Resources of a Region (PAGE 57)	Economically Speaking (PAGE 58)	Life Cycle Protection (PAGE 59)
MATH																		
Computation	•			•	•	•												
Data Analysis and Probability			•															
Number and Operations	•			•	•	•												
Problem Solving	•	•	•	•	•	•												
Telling Time		•																
SCIENCE																		
The Characteristics of Organisms							•	•	•	•	•	•						
Investigation and Experimentation							•	•				•						
Life Cycles of Organisms							•	•	•	•	•	•						
Organisms and Their Environment							•		•			•						
SOCIAL STUDIES																		
Ancestors													•					
Community														•				
Economics															•	•	•	
Government														•				•
Map Skills																•		

Introducing . . . Life Cycles

FACTS ABOUT LIFE CYCLES

- All living things have a life cycle.
- Most life cycles begin with a seed, an egg, or a live birth.
- A life cycle is different for plants and animals.
- Insect life cycles are short, often less than a year.
- Most animal life cycles last over a period of many years.

ASSESSMENT ANSWERS

Life Cycles Pretest (PAGE 9)
1. *a* 2. *a* 3. *b* 4. *a* 5. *a* 6. *a* 7. *d* 8. *b*

Life Cycles—Reading Comprehension Test (PAGES 11–12)
1. *b* 2. *a* 3. *a* 4. *c* 5. *d* 6. *c*

Life Cycles Cumulative Test (PAGES 62–63)
1. *d* 2. *b* 3. *b* 4. *d* 5. *a* 6. *a* 7. *b* 8. *c* 9. *c* 10. *b* 11. *Answers may vary*
12. *Answers may vary*

LITERATURE LINKS

The Carrot Seed by Ruth Krauss (HarperCollins)

From Seed to Plant by Gail Gibbons (Holiday House)

The Great Kapok Tree: A Tale of the Amazon Rain Forest by Lynn Cherry (Harcourt)

How Do Birds Find Their Way? by Roma Gans (HarperCollins)

Life Cycles by Michael Elsohn Ross (The Millbrook Press)

The Magic School Bus Plants Seeds: A Book About How Living Things Grow by Joanna Cole (Scholastic)

Monarch Butterfly by David M. Schwartz (Creative Teaching Press)

Our Animal Friends at Maple Hill Farm by Alice and Martin Provensen (Aladdin)

Pumpkin Circle: The Story of a Garden by George Levenson (Ten Speed Press)

This Year's Garden by Cynthia Rylant (Simon & Schuster)

The Tiny Seed by Eric Carle (Simon & Schuster)

Waiting for Wings by Lois Ehlert (Harcourt)

Wood Frog by David M. Schwartz (Creative Teaching Press)

VOCABULARY

adult	develop
egg	larva
life cycle	mature
metamorphosis	offspring
pupa	stage

Name_____ Date_____

Life Cycles Pretest

Directions: Fill in the best answer for each question.

1 True or False: Bees help to continue the life cycle of some plants.

   ⓐ true

   ⓑ false

2 True or False: The life cycle of most insects lasts less than a year.

   ⓐ true

   ⓑ false

3 True or False: Rabbits lay eggs.

   ⓐ true

   ⓑ false

4 True or False: The life cycle of a frog begins with an egg.

   ⓐ true

   ⓑ false

5 Which of the following does not have a life cycle?

   ⓐ car

   ⓑ grasshopper

   ⓒ tomato

   ⓓ tiger

6 Which mammal's life cycle benefits humans?

   ⓐ cow

   ⓑ honeybee

   ⓒ lizard

   ⓓ all of the above

7 Which statement is true?

   ⓐ A tadpole grows up to be a fish.

   ⓑ A duckling grows up to be a chicken.

   ⓒ A pumpkin seed grows to become a zucchini plant.

   ⓓ A caterpillar grows up to be a butterfly.

8 Where could you look to find information about the life cycle of a mouse?

   ⓐ dictionary

   ⓑ encyclopedia

   ⓒ comic book

   ⓓ cookbook

What Do You Know? KWL Chart

What We Know	What We Want to Know	What We Learned

Name_____   Date_____

Life Cycles—
Reading Comprehension Test

Directions: Read the story and then answer the six questions.

A life cycle keeps repeating itself. It is like a circle story. It is sometimes called the "circle of life." A life cycle begins with an egg, a seed, or a baby. The egg hatches. The seed sprouts. Or, the baby is born. Then, the egg, seed, or baby grows up. Finally, it helps create a new egg, seed, or baby so the circle of life can go on. Each living thing has a life cycle.

The life cycle of a frog begins with an egg. The egg hatches into a tadpole. The tadpole lives in the water. It breathes with gills and has a tail. The tadpole forms lungs and legs as it grows. When this happens, the gills and tail go away. It is now a froglet. The froglet loses its tail and grows into a frog. Now that it is a frog, it lives mostly on land. Then, the frog lays eggs to repeat the life cycle.

The life cycle of many plants begins with a seed. The seed becomes a sprout. The sprout grows into a plant. The plant matures. Then, it makes more seeds. Those seeds can be planted to begin the life cycle again.

Every living thing has a life cycle. Look all around you. What is the life cycle of each living thing that you see?

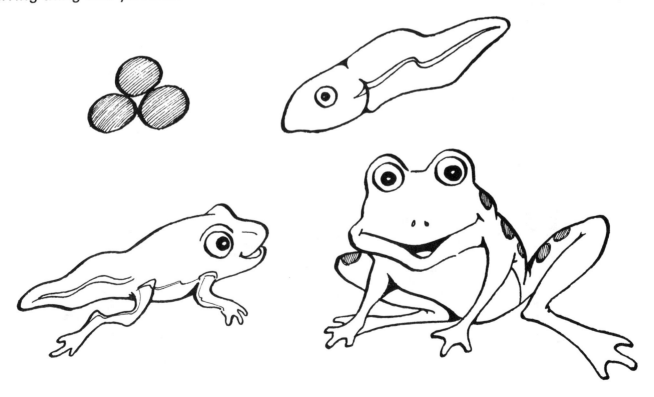

Name_____ Date_____

Life Cycles—
Reading Comprehension Test

1 A life cycle includes . . .

ⓐ everything we eat and drink.

ⓑ the stages of life a plant, an animal, or a human goes through.

ⓒ an egg at the beginning of each first stage.

ⓓ none of the above

2 True or False: Every living thing has a life cycle.

ⓐ true

ⓑ false

3 Which is the correct life cycle of a frog?

ⓐ egg, tadpole, froglet, frog

ⓑ frog, tadpole, egg, froglet

ⓒ egg, froglet, tadpole, frog

ⓓ egg, frog, froglet, tadpole

4 Which is the correct life cycle of a plant?

ⓐ seed, plant, sprout

ⓑ sprout, plant, seed

ⓒ seed, sprout, plant

ⓓ plant, sprout, seed

5 Which of the following does not have a life cycle?

ⓐ turtle

ⓑ person

ⓒ cactus

ⓓ water

6 Which statement about the life cycle of a frog is false?

ⓐ The egg hatches into a tadpole.

ⓑ A froglet will lose its tail.

ⓒ A frog lives mostly in the water.

ⓓ A tadpole forms lungs and legs as it grows.

Language Arts

Researching a Life Cycle

- *Life Cycles* by Michael Elsohn Ross
- Life Cycles transparency
- Life Cycles Research reproducible (page 22)
- overhead projector
- reference materials

OBJECTIVES

Students will
- learn the life cycle of a chosen plant or animal.
- understand how to use reference materials to find information.

Read *Life Cycles* to the class, and discuss the life cycles of a plant, a butterfly, and a person. Remind students that all living things have a life cycle. Display the Life Cycles transparency, and discuss the different life cycles shown. Brainstorm with the class numerous plants and animals. List student responses on the board. Tell students that they will select a plant or an animal from the board and research its life cycle. Give each student a Life Cycles Research reproducible. Have students write the name of the plant or animal on the first line. Have students use research materials such as encyclopedias or the Internet to find information about their plant or animal. Encourage them to determine how their plant or animal started (e.g., from a seed, egg, or live birth), where it grows (e.g., in water, within its mother), what it needs to grow (e.g., food, sunlight), and what it looks like as it changes (e.g., a tadpole has a tail that shrinks as it turns into a froglet). Challenge students to use their notes to write on a separate piece of paper an essay about their plant or animal. Ask them to include as many details as possible. Encourage volunteers to read their essay to the class.

- Dolphin Delivery reproducible (page 23)
- crayons or markers

Dolphin Delivery

OBJECTIVE

- Students will add correct capitalization and commas to a story.

Ask students to share with the class facts they know about dolphins. Prompt students to say that dolphins live in the ocean, are mammals and not fish, and are very smart. Review with students the rules for capitalization and commas. For example, people's names and the names of cities are capitalized. Words in a list are separated by commas. Where a city and state are listed, a comma separates the city from the state. Give each student a Dolphin Delivery reproducible. Explain to students that the person who wrote the Dolphin Delivery story needs their help to capitalize names and add commas to separate words in a list as well as dates and cities and states. Read the story aloud. Encourage students to reread the story silently or with a partner and then make the necessary corrections. Invite students to correctly rewrite the story on another piece of paper. Invite students to illustrate their completed paper. Students should capitalize 14 words and add six commas to the story.

A Friendly Letter from the Farm

MATERIALS

● *Our Animal Friends at Maple Hill Farm*
  by Alice and Martin Provensen

● chart paper

OBJECTIVE

● Students will write a friendly letter.

Read *Our Animal Friends at Maple Hill Farm* to the class. Discuss the different animals that lived on the farm. Review with students how to write a friendly letter, including how to correctly write the date, salutation, body, closing, and signature. As a class, write on a piece of chart paper a friendly letter to the farmer at Maple Hill Farm asking if you can visit the farm in the springtime. After completing the letter, have students imagine that they have just spent a week or two at the Maple Hill Farm. Brainstorm with the class the life cycle of one or more of the animals from the story. Have each student write a friendly letter to a classmate or friend and describe his or her experience with the animals at the farm. Have students include the life cycle of at least one farm animal in their letter. Remind them to include all the parts of a friendly letter. Invite volunteers to share their letter with the class. Display the letters on a bulletin board titled *Our Trip to the Farm.*

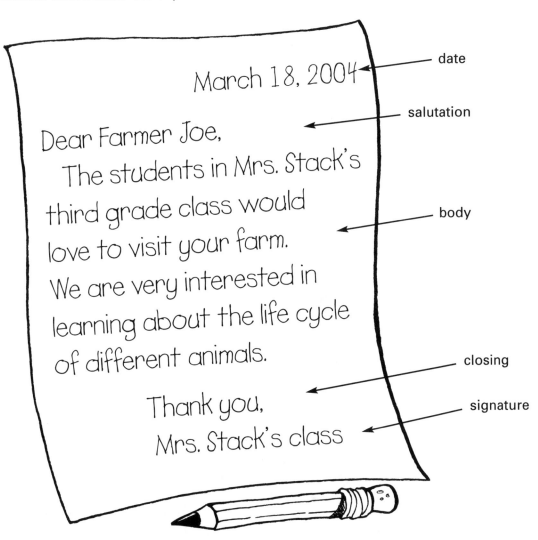

March 18, 2004 ← date

Dear Farmer Joe, ← salutation
 The students in Mrs. Stack's third grade class would love to visit your farm. ← body
We are very interested in learning about the life cycle of different animals.

Thank you, ← closing
 Mrs. Stack's class ← signature

- Watching the Cycle of Life reproducible (page 24)
- crayons or markers
- bookbinding materials

Watching the Cycle of Life

OBJECTIVE

● Students will write declarative, interrogative, imperative, and exclamatory sentences.

Review with students the four types of sentences: declarative, interrogative, imperative, and exclamatory. Give each student a Watching the Cycle of Life reproducible, and encourage students to discuss the pictures on the page. Invite them to imagine what the people in the four boxes are saying. Have students write a different type of sentence in each speech bubble to tell a story that matches the pictures. Invite them to color the pictures. Bind the completed pages in a book titled *Watching the Cycle of Life.*

MATERIALS

- A Spider Is Born reproducible (page 25)

A Spider Is Born

OBJECTIVE

● Students will develop vocabulary by completing a cloze activity.

Brainstorm with students facts about spiders such as *spiders have eight legs* and *they are arachnids.* Record student responses on the board. Tell students they are going to read an incomplete story about the life cycle of spiders. They need to use words from the word bank to complete the story. Give each student an A Spider Is Born reproducible. Invite volunteers to read aloud the words from the word bank. Make sure students understand the meaning of each word and then read aloud the incomplete story. Then, ask students to reread the story silently or with a partner and determine which word fits best on each line to complete the story. Have students write a word in each blank. Encourage them to use context clues to help determine which word choice is best. Have students reread the story to make sure it makes sense. Students should write these words, in the following order, to complete the story: *eight, eggs, sac, weather, hatchling, web, insects, oil, molting,* and *cycle.*

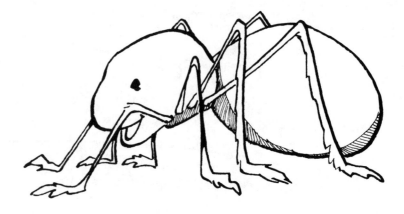

Can You Find the Word?

MATERIALS

● Can You Find the Word? reproducible (page 26)

OBJECTIVE

● Students will develop vocabulary by searching for correctly spelled words related to life cycles.

Give each student a Can You Find the Word? reproducible. Invite volunteers to read aloud the words at the bottom of the page and share the meaning of each word. Discuss how the words relate to life cycles. Explain to students that they will look for words horizontally, vertically, and diagonally in the puzzle. Model how to draw a circle around a word on the board. Explain that once students find a word in the puzzle, they should draw a circle around the entire word, making sure not to cover any other letters in the puzzle. When students are finished, invite them to switch papers with a classmate. Have the classmate double-check that all chosen words are correct and then return the paper to its owner. To extend the activity, have students create a story using as many words from the word bank as possible.

Repeating Rimes in Word Family Words

MATERIALS

● Flowers reproducible (page 27)

OBJECTIVES

Students will
● identify rimes.
● create rhyming words.

Give each student a Flowers reproducible. Have volunteers read aloud the words on the reproducible. Discuss the meaning of each word. Share with the class how the words relate to life cycles. Tell students to circle the rime (all of the sounds that follow the first consonant or consonant blend) in each word. Explain to the class that they can create rhyming words by changing the beginning sound of the given word. For example, for the word *sprout,* a student could write *about, pout, stout,* and *shout.* Invite students to create rhyming words for the word on each flower. Have them write the rhyming words on the petals of the flower. Encourage students to repeat this process with the remaining three words. To extend the activity, write other word family words on additional flowers.

Connecting a Caterpillar

MATERIALS

- *Waiting for Wings* by Lois Ehlert
- Connecting a Caterpillar reproducible (page 28)
- colored copy paper
- construction paper
- scissors
- glue
- crayons or markers

OBJECTIVES

Students will
- extend their life cycle vocabulary.
- place words in alphabetical order.
- identify the number of syllables in words.

Copy a class set of the Connecting a Caterpillar reproducible on assorted colors of paper. Read *Waiting for Wings* to the class, and discuss the life cycle of a caterpillar. Give each student a Connecting a Caterpillar reproducible and a piece of construction paper. Tell students that a caterpillar's body has 13 segments and 14 legs. Invite students to read aloud the words on the reproducible. Discuss with the class the meaning of each word. Have students cut out the circles and glue them in alphabetical order on their construction paper. Encourage them to use crayons or markers to add facial features, antennae, and 14 legs to their caterpillar. To extend the activity, review syllabication with students. Ask them to write the number of syllables each word has under the word.

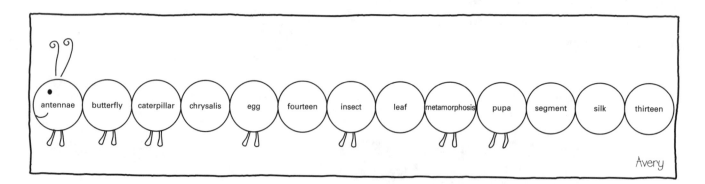

Get the Idea?

OBJECTIVES

Students will
- identify the main idea and details of a passage.
- paraphrase the main idea and details of a passage.

Copy a class set of the Beehive and the Life Cycle of a Bee reproducibles. Give each student both reproducibles and two colored pencils. Discuss with students what the main idea of a paragraph is. Read aloud the passage about bees from the Life Cycle of a Bee reproducible. Have students use the blue pencil to underline the main idea. Discuss which sentence they underlined. Have students paraphrase the underlined sentence and write it on the bee on the Beehive reproducible. Tell them to return to the passage and use the red pencil to underline three details that support the main idea. Invite volunteers to share their underlined sentences. Have students paraphrase these sentences and write them on the hive on the Beehive reproducible. Give each student a piece of construction paper. Ask students to cut out their beehive with the bee and glue it to their construction paper. Invite volunteers to share their work with the class.

Beehive

The queen bee has the greatest responsibility.

The queen bee lays eggs to begin the new life cycle of the bee. The eggs hatch and grow into three types of bees. They can be workers, drones, or males. Each bee has a specific role. The bee's life cycle consists of an egg, larva, pupa, and adult.

Cycling Together

OBJECTIVE

● Students will identify cause and effect sentences in a paragraph.

Explain to the class that the life cycle of one plant or animal may affect the life cycle of another plant or animal. For example, flowers are dependent on bees to spread their pollen. Tell students that they will be reading a paragraph about the life cycles of bees and plants. Divide the class into pairs. Give each pair of students a Cause and Effect reproducible. Have students read the paragraph at the top of the page. Then, as a class, brainstorm some cause scenarios of the life cycle of a bee and the life cycle of a plant. Record student responses on the board. Then, have students list the cause scenarios from the board on their paper and write an effect scenario for each cause. For example, students might write *pollen from one plant is transferred to another* as a cause and *a new plant will grow* as the effect. Encourage students to list as many causes and effects from the paragraph as possible. Invite partners to share their list with the class.

Life Cycle Sounds

OBJECTIVE

● Students will use alliteration in sentences.

Write the following sentences on the chalkboard:
Baby bunnies are buried beneath branches when born.
It takes some time for tiny tadpoles to lose their tails.
Some seeds sprout into stiff celery stalks.
The happy hen hopes her chicks will hatch in a hurry.

Read each sentence to the class. Then, reread each sentence and pause to ask students to describe what they heard. Explain that each sentence features *alliteration,* which is the repetition of words that begin with the same sound. Invite the class to choose another plant or animal. Write the name of the plant or animal on the board. Brainstorm words that begin with the same beginning sound as the name. Remind students that the words need to relate to the plant or animal. Then, have them write an alliterative sentence about the plant or animal and draw a picture of it above their sentence. Challenge students to write an alliterative sentence about the plant or animal's life cycle. Invite volunteers to share their sentences with the class.

Growing Up

MATERIALS

- *The Giving Tree* by Shel Silverstein (HarperCollins)
- overhead projector/transparency
- drawing paper

OBJECTIVES

Students will
- use prior knowledge to help determine the life cycle of specific characters from a story.
- compare and contrast the life of two characters from a story.

Draw a line down the center of a transparency to make two columns. Title the first column *The Man* and the second column *The Tree.* Read aloud *The Giving Tree.* Invite students to describe how the young boy in the story grows to be an old man. Write the stages of the man's life in the left column on the transparency. Invite students to describe how the tree grows in the story. Write students' ideas in the right column on the transparency. Challenge students to use the information on the transparency to develop sentences that compare and contrast the stages of the boy's life and the stages of the tree's life. For example, a student could say *When the boy became a grown man, the tree was full of ripe apples.* List students' responses on the transparency. Give each student a piece of drawing paper. Invite students to select the boy or the tree and list in a circle the life cycle of the chosen character. Remind students to use prior knowledge to add any stages that were not previously mentioned in the story.

Name_____ Date_____

Life Cycles Research

Name of Plant or Animal _____

How It Started	Where It Grows

What It Needs to Grow	What It Looks Like as It Changes

Name_____ Date_____

Dolphin Delivery

Directions: The author of this story needs your help capitalizing names of people and places and adding commas to lists of items and between dates, cities, and states. Read the story and make the needed corrections.

The dapin city zoo reports that a new dolphin pup was born on may 17 2003. The baby's mother, seabreeze, was born in the Atlantic Ocean and came to the zoo six years ago.

A dolphin may look like a fish, but it is really a mammal. It is a mammal because it is born live from its mother it drinks its mother's milk and it breathes air.

When a dolphin pup is born, it stays near its mother for two to six years. A dolphin pup's mother will teach it how to search for food escape animals that might harm it and determine where it is safe to sleep.

Dolphins are very smart. They move their bodies in special ways. They make sounds with their blowhole to "talk" with each other.

The new dolphin pup will need a name. Can you think of one? If so, write to chris, one of the zookeepers at the zoo. Here is the address:

dapin city zoo

1415 seaside drive

dapin city florida 91919

Please visit the new dolphin during regular zoo hours!

Watching the Cycle of Life

Directions: Imagine what the people in the four boxes are saying. Write a different type of sentence in each speech bubble to tell a story that matches the pictures.

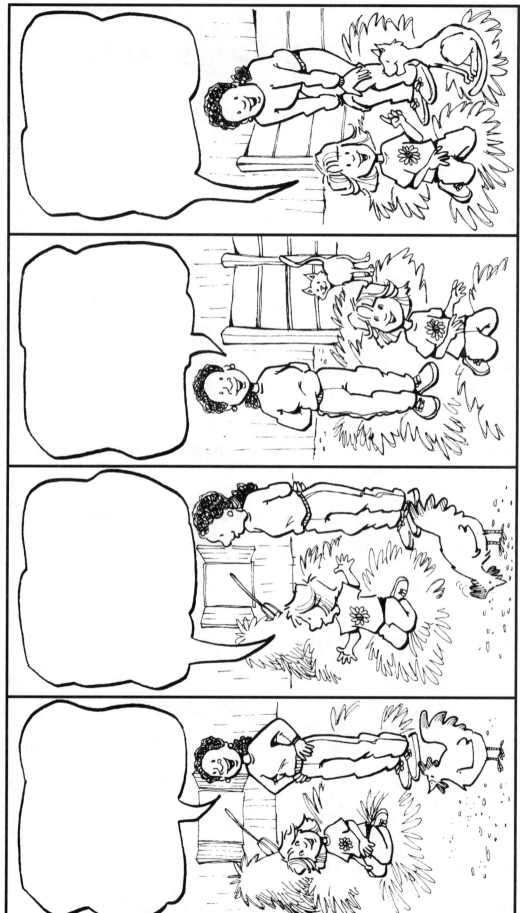

Name_____ Date_____

A Spider Is Born

Directions: Use the words from the word bank to complete the story. Reread your completed story to make sure it makes sense.

Word Bank				
hatchling	weather	web	sac	eggs
cycle	oil	eight	molting	insects

Spiders are part of the arachnid group. They have _____ legs and are

born from _____. Most female spiders lay a large number of eggs because

many of the eggs will die or be eaten. When a spider lays her eggs, she spins a silk

egg _____ around them. Here the eggs are protected from cold and

rainy _____.

When a baby spider hatches it is called a _____ or a nymph. The

babies remain in the egg sacs until they are able to see and move well enough to catch

their own food to eat.

Many spiders catch their food by spinning a _____. The webs are

made from sticky silken threads that trap _____ that fly into them. A spider

cannot get stuck in its own web because its body is covered with a slippery _____.

As a spider grows, it will shed its outer skin many times. This is called

_____. The life _____ of a spider continues when the hatchling

is old enough to lay her own eggs.

Life Cycles © 2003 Creative Teaching Press

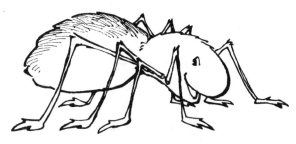

Can You Find the Word?

Directions: Ten life cycle words are hidden in the puzzle below. Circle each word as you find it. Words can be forward, backward, up, down, or diagonal.

l	e	d	e	v	e	a	d	q	l	m	h	d
p	i	o	f	f	l	c	e	o	a	a	l	s
r	g	f	r	i	a	t	v	s	r	t	i	e
i	p	r	e	f	r	h	e	t	v	s	f	v
a	p	u	p	c	v	l	l	p	o	u	e	e
o	d	l	y	c	a	l	o	h	f	r	c	l
f	e	i	t	s	l	l	p	e	f	e	y	l
f	v	f	l	g	r	r	e	g	s	s	c	a
s	e	e	u	s	o	r	t	h	p	t	l	g
d	t	c	d	m	p	u	p	l	r	a	e	e
b	r	g	a	d	u	l	a	l	i	p	t	x
g	o	t	h	s	q	a	g	g	n	e	r	s
l	e	g	g	p	a	s	t	a	g	e	t	r
m	p	s	t	r	v	e	r	u	t	a	m	w

Word Bank

adult	develop	egg	larva	life cycle
mature	metamorphosis	offspring	pupa	stage

Name_____ Date_____

Flowers

Connecting a Caterpillar

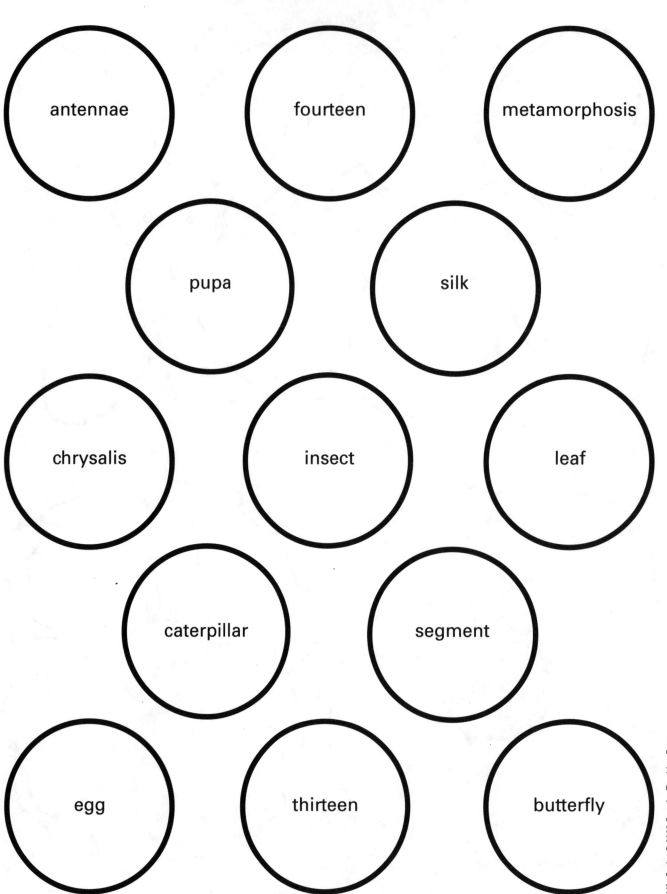

antennae

fourteen

metamorphosis

pupa

silk

chrysalis

insect

leaf

caterpillar

segment

egg

thirteen

butterfly

Beehive

Life Cycle of a Bee

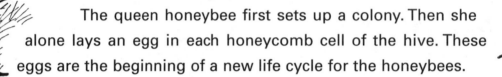

The queen honeybee first sets up a colony. Then she alone lays an egg in each honeycomb cell of the hive. These eggs are the beginning of a new life cycle for the honeybees.

The eggs may hatch and grow into one of three types of bees: female workers, drones, or males. A new queen is born usually when the colony gets very big or if something happens to the old queen.

When a bee hatches from its egg, it is called a larva. The only thing a larva does is eat and grow. The larva will molt, or shed its skin, five times. Then it spins a cocoon. At this stage, the bee is called a pupa.

After eight to ten days, the pupa emerges as an adult bee. The honeybee cycle continues. The adult bee may collect nectar and pollen or feed a new group of developing larvae to help the colony survive.

Life Cycles © 2003 Creative Teaching Press

Cause and Effect

For a new plant to grow, a seed must be created. This is done when pollen from one plant is transferred to another plant. The wind might blow pollen from one flower to another, or an insect may carry pollen from one flower to another. A sugary liquid called nectar and bright petals attract bees to a flower. Bees use nectar to make honey. When a bee lands on a flower to collect the nectar, some of the pollen attaches to its body. When the bee travels to a different flower to collect more nectar, it drops some of the pollen on the flower. This may cause a new flower to form.

Cause

_____

_____

_____

_____

_____

_____

_____

Effect

_____

_____

_____

_____

_____

_____

_____

Math

Life Cycle Math

MATERIALS

● Life Cycle Math reproducible (page 36)

OBJECTIVE

● Students will use computation strategies to solve word problems.

Tell students that every living thing has a life cycle but different things happen during each living thing's life. For example, a kitten and a guinea pig are both born live from their mother. The guinea pig goes through its life cycle in approximately three years while a cat goes through its life cycle in about fourteen years. Give each student a Life Cycle Math reproducible. Tell students to use their computation skills to solve the problems. Invite volunteers to share their answers with the class.

A Time to Grow

MATERIALS

● Egg Hatching reproducible (page 37)

OBJECTIVE

● Students will tell time to the quarter of an hour.

Ask students *How are chicks born?* Prompt students to say that chicks hatch from eggs. Give each student an Egg Hatching reproducible. Invite students to read the sentence and the time on the clock below each picture. Have students write the time shown on each clock on the corresponding line. Explain to students that each clock is an example of what might happen during the life cycle of a chicken. Tell students that actual times may vary. Review the answers with the class.

At __3:45__, the hen lays an egg.

Measuring My Garden

MATERIALS

- Measuring My Garden reproducible (page 38)
- seed packets—for plants no larger than 2' (61 cm)
- construction paper
- crayons or markers
- bookbinding materials

OBJECTIVE

● Students will create a bar graph from information provided on seed packets.

Share with the class various types of seeds, and discuss what the seeds will look like once they mature. Explain to students that they will read the back of their seed packet to determine how tall their plant will grow. Divide the class into small groups. Give each student a Measuring My Garden reproducible, and give each group five different seed packets. Tell students to write the name of each type of seed in the bottom row of each column on their reproducible. Have students shade in the corresponding number of boxes to match the height the plant will reach. When groups have completed their graph, give each group a large piece of construction paper. Have group members draw what their garden will look like according to the measurements recorded on their graph. Collect each group's drawing, and bind the pages into a class book titled *Our Class Garden.*

Spiderweb Math

MATERIALS

- Spiderweb Math reproducible (page 39)
- lamination materials (optional)
- markers (e.g., chips, beans, plastic spider and fly)

OBJECTIVE

● Students will use problem-solving strategies to compete against an opponent.

Make a copy of the Spiderweb Math reproducible. Write addition, subtraction, multiplication, and/or division problems on the reproducible. Copy the revised reproducible for each pair of students. As an option, laminate the reproducibles for durability. Explain to the class that many spiders catch their prey in webs made of fine, silky threads. Spiderwebs come in various shapes and designs. Some spiders just weave an irregular mass of silk threads. Web-spinning spiders usually construct their web and wait for an insect to crawl into it. Divide the class into pairs. Give each pair a prepared game board and two game markers. Have one player, the "spider," place his or her marker in the middle of the web. Have the other player, the "fly," place a marker in any other section of the web. Tell partners they will take turns selecting a math problem in a space adjacent to their current position. If they solve the problem, they move to that space. If not, they stay where they are. The object of the game is for the fly to cross the web before the spider catches it. Players can move in any direction on the web.

Numbers in Nature

OBJECTIVES

Students will
● use statistical information about the life cycle of specific plants and animals.
● create word problems about the life cycle of specific plants and animals.

Write the following information on the chalkboard:

Most kangaroos can leap 25 feet (8 meters) in a single jump.

A caterpillar is fully grown about two weeks after hatching from an egg.

A ladybug larva can eat about 50 aphids a day.

A mother sea horse lays her eggs in the father sea horse's pouch. 100 baby sea horses will emerge about a month later.

Invite volunteers to read aloud the sentences. Divide the class into pairs. Have partners use the statistical information from the board to create at least five word problems. For example, students could write *How many times did the kangaroo jump if it went 100 feet?* or *How far would a kangaroo go in three jumps?* Have students write their questions on a piece of paper and write the answers on the back of their paper. Invite partners to trade papers with another pair of students and solve the other students' problems. Then, have students check each other's work. To extend learning, invite students to skim through reference books about life cycles to find statistical facts about other plants and animals, and have them use the information to write problems.

Life Cycle of a Frog

MATERIALS

- Life Cycle of a Frog Cards (page 40)
- Life Cycle of a Frog Game Board (page 41)
- scissors
- resealable plastic bags
- dice
- markers (e.g., beans, circular chips)
- scratch paper

OBJECTIVE

- Students will use problem-solving strategies to help them learn facts about the life cycle of frogs.

Copy a set of the Life Cycle of a Frog Cards and a Game Board for each pair of students. Cut apart each set, and place them in a resealable plastic bag. Tell students they will play a game based on the life cycle of a frog. Divide the class into pairs. Give each pair of students a game board, a set of cards, a die, two different markers, and a piece of scratch paper. Have the first student roll the die. Have the student's partner draw a card and read it aloud. The first student will solve the math problem on the card in order to move ahead the corresponding number of spaces on the game board. If the student does not correctly solve the math problem on the card, he or she does not move ahead. Have the student's partner check the answer (located in the upper right corner of the card) to make sure it is correct. Have students continue reading and solving problems until one player reaches the finish and wins the game. To extend the activity, have students create their own math questions and replay the game using the new questions.

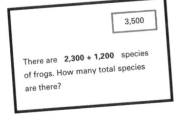

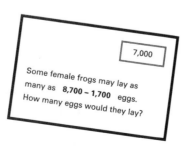

Life Cycle Math

Directions: Solve each problem.

1 Most snakes lay eggs. If one snake lays three eggs and two more snakes each lay four eggs, how many total eggs will they lay?

_____

2 If a guinea pig's life cycle lasts three years and a cat's life cycle lasts fourteen years, how many more years is the cat's life cycle than the guinea pig's life cycle?

_____

3 If a rabbit had a litter once a year for five years and there were four kits or kittens in each litter, how many total kits or kittens would the rabbit have?

_____

4 If it takes one month for an insect to go through each of its four stages of life, how many total months will it take the insect to complete its entire life cycle?

_____

Name_____   Date_____

Egg Hatching

Directions: Use the information shown on the clocks to complete each statement. Actual times may vary.

At _____, the hen lays an egg.

At _____, the chick is growing inside the egg.

At _____, the chick begins to peck on the shell.

At _____, the chick emerges from the egg.

At _____, the chick cannot walk yet.

At _____, the chick can walk!

Name_____   Date_____

 # Measuring My Garden

Directions: Write the names of your seeds at the bottom of the graph. Use the information on your seed packets to determine how tall each plant will grow and record this data on the graph.

24 inches (61 cm)					
22 inches (56 cm)					
20 inches (51 cm)					
18 inches (46 cm)					
16 inches (40.5 cm)					
14 inches (36 cm)					
12 inches (30.5 cm)					
10 inches (25.5 cm)					
8 inches (20 cm)					
6 inches (15 cm)					
4 inches (10 cm)					
2 inches (5 cm)					

Spiderweb Math

Life Cycle of a Frog Cards

3,500	7,000
There are **2,300 + 1,200** species of frogs. How many total species are there?	Some female frogs may lay as many as **8,700 – 1,700** eggs. How many eggs would they lay?

10	5
It takes about **2 + 3 + 2 + 1 + 2** days for the tadpole to be ready to wiggle out of the egg. How many days does it take?	Tadpoles breathe through gills on the outside of their body for about **28 – 23** weeks. How many weeks do they breathe through gills?

5	1
After **15 – 10** weeks, the tadpole's back legs begin to appear and the outside gills begin to disappear. How many weeks does this take?	In about **30 – 29** week(s) after the back legs have appeared, the tadpole develops lungs and breathes air. How many weeks does this take?

10 to 12	3½
At about **6 + 4 to 4 + 4 + 4** weeks, the tadpole grows front legs. How many weeks is this?	After about **20 – 17 + ½** months, the tadpole has become a froglet and is ready to eat small bugs and spend time out of the water. How many months does this take?

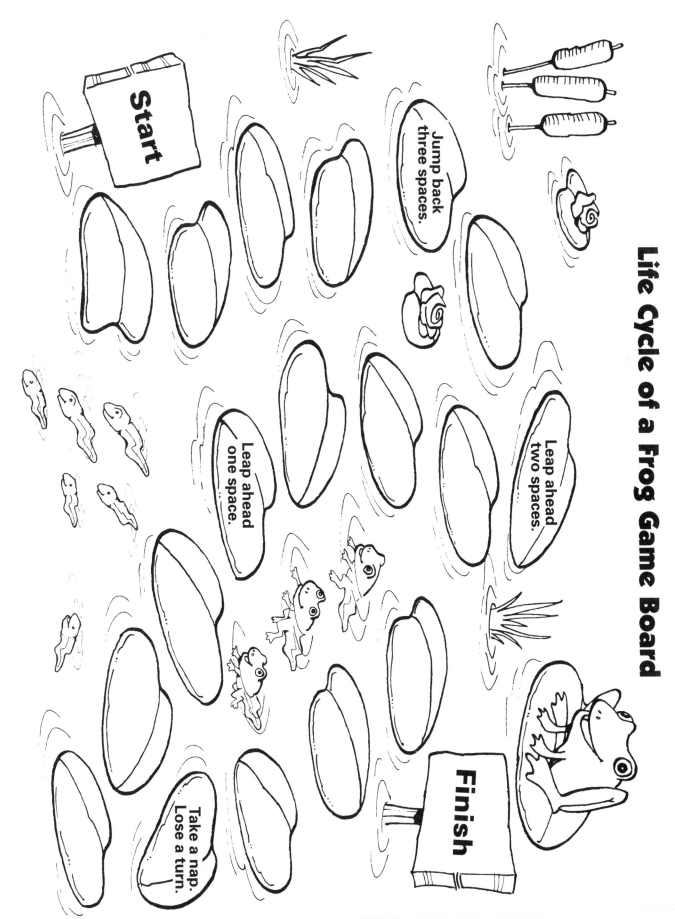

Life Cycle of a Frog Game Board

Start

Jump back three spaces.

Leap ahead one space.

Leap ahead two spaces.

Take a nap. Lose a turn.

Finish

Science

The Carrot Seed

OBJECTIVE

- Students will compare the growth of a plant near sunlight to a plant that is away from sunlight.

MATERIALS

- *The Carrot Seed* by Ruth Krauss
- The Growth of My Plant reproducible (page 47)
- Life Cycles transparency
- overhead projector
- carrot seeds
- chart paper
- small cups
- potting soil
- permanent markers
- water
- rulers

Read *The Carrot Seed* to the class, and discuss how the boy's dedication to the seed helped it grow. Ask students what they think a plant needs to grow. Encourage students to share that a plant needs sunlight and water to grow. Display the Life Cycles transparency. Review with the class the life cycle of a plant. Hold up a carrot seed, and ask students to whisper to the student on their right side what stage of the life cycle the carrot seed is. Tell students that they are going to plant carrot seeds to determine what helps them grow. Ask students to predict if the carrot will grow faster near a window or away from a window. Record their predictions on a piece of chart paper. Divide the class into pairs. Give each pair of students two small cups, some potting soil, several carrot seeds, and a permanent marker. Ask students to use the marker to write their names on their cups and label one cup *A* and the other cup *B*. Tell them to fill their cups halfway with soil and plant a few seeds in each cup. Remind students to slightly cover their seeds with additional soil. Explain that if the seeds are buried too deeply they will not sprout. Have students water their soil and place one cup near a window and the other away from a window. (Note: Carrot seeds sometimes take as long as three weeks to sprout and must be kept moist at all times.) Give each student a The Growth of My Plant reproducible. Ask students to use a ruler to measure the growth of their plants each day and record the number in the appropriate column on their reproducible. Have them record in the "Comments" section any changes they notice with their plants. Encourage students to hypothesize as to why the plant that is away from the window is not growing at the same rate as the plant near the window. Once the plants have reached a determined height, review with the class the stage the plants are currently in.

Life Cycle Mobiles

OBJECTIVE

- Students will use research materials to learn about the life cycle of an animal.

Explain to the class that they are going to create a mobile that shows the life cycle of a chosen animal. Divide the class into pairs. Give each pair of students four to five index cards, yarn, and a hole punch. Brainstorm with the class different animals. Record student responses on the board. Discuss with students where they could learn more about an animal. Have each pair select an animal. Encourage students to use reference materials and/or the Internet to learn about the life cycle of their animal. Ask them to write a description of each stage of their animal's life cycle on a separate index card. Have them illustrate the life cycle stage on the back of the card. Ask students to title an additional index card *Life Cycle of a (Animal's Name)* and write their names on the card. Then, have students punch a hole in the bottom of the title card and a hole in the top and bottom of the remaining cards. Tell them to use yarn to attach the index cards in the correct sequence to show the animal's life cycle. Display the completed mobiles around the classroom.

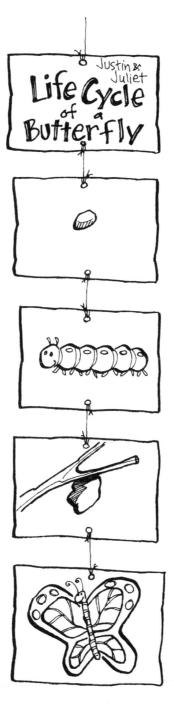

Life Cycle Circles

OBJECTIVE

● Students will learn about the life cycle of a wood frog.

Explain to the class that there are many different types of frogs but the stages of their life cycles are similar. All frogs begin as tiny eggs laid in water; hatch into tadpoles; undergo metamorphosis, developing legs and lungs to replace their tail and gills; and emerge as adult frogs. Read *Wood Frog* to the class, and discuss with students the frog's metamorphosis and the coloration and dark eye mask typical of all wood frogs. Give each student a copy of both Life Cycle Wheel reproducibles and a brass fastener. Have students draw a picture that matches the sentence(s) in each section of page 49 and color both pages. Have them cut out both parts of the life cycle wheel and use the brass fastener to poke a hole at the dot on the top wheel and at the intersection of the lines on the bottom wheel. Show students how to insert the brass fastener into the hole in the top circle and through the bottom circle and open the fastener flat on the back. Have students write their name on the front of the wheel. Invite them to turn the wheel to observe the stages of the life cycle of a wood frog and read the stages to a partner.

MATERIALS

● *Wood Frog* by David M. Schwartz
● Life Cycle Wheel reproducibles (pages 48–49)
● brass fasteners
● crayons or markers
● scissors

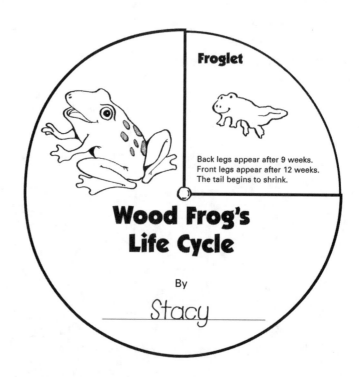

Froglet

Back legs appear after 9 weeks.
Front legs appear after 12 weeks.
The tail begins to shrink.

Wood Frog's Life Cycle

By

Stacy

Life Cycle Memory

MATERIALS

- Life Cycle Memory Cards (pages 50–51)
- card stock
- scissors
- resealable plastic bags

OBJECTIVE

- Students will identify the life cycle of a frog, butterfly, human, and plant.

Copy a set of Life Cycle Memory Cards onto card stock for each pair of students. Cut apart the cards, and place each set in a resealable plastic bag. Review with the class the life cycle of a frog, butterfly, human, and plant. Record the stages on the board. Divide the class into pairs. Give each pair of students a set of cards. Have students place the cards facedown in rows. Tell students that they will play a memory game. Explain to the class that partners will take turns turning four cards faceup. If students turn over all four cards for the life cycle of a frog, butterfly, human, or plant, they keep all four cards. If the four cards do not complete the same life cycle, students turn the cards facedown in their original location. Play continues with students taking turns trying to uncover all four cards for one life cycle. The student who collects the most cards wins the game. To extend the activity, invite students to take turns selecting a card and trying to name the complete life cycle without looking at any other cards.

Baby Basics

MATERIALS

- Animal Life Cycle Cards (page 52)
- construction paper
- scissors
- glue

OBJECTIVE

- Students will match common attributes of different animals.

Give each student a set of Animal Life Cycle Cards and a piece of construction paper. Have students cut apart their cards and sort them into two groups: life cycle description cards and animal picture cards. Invite students to read each description card, match it to the corresponding animal card, and write the animal's name in the blank. Once students have matched the four pairs of cards, ask them to glue the cards on their construction paper.

A _____ does not have any fur. It cannot see or hear at first.

The Life of a Butterfly

OBJECTIVE

- Students will learn about the stages of the life cycle of a butterfly.

Read *Monarch Butterfly* to the class, and discuss the life of a monarch butterfly. Explain to the class that a butterfly's life cycle includes many changes over a short period of time, called metamorphosis. This metamorphosis involves four stages: egg, larva (caterpillar), pupa (chrysalis), and adult butterfly. Explain that for most adult butterflies, life is very short, usually only a few weeks. However, the monarch butterfly lives for about two years. Give each student a Butterfly Life Cycle reproducible and some sesame seeds. Have students color the leaf, branch, and adult butterfly and then glue several seeds onto the leaf to represent butterfly eggs. Demonstrate for the class how to make a monarch caterpillar (in its larva stage) by holding black, white, and yellow pipe cleaner pieces against a pencil with your thumb and fingers, completely winding the pieces around the pencil with your other hand, and removing the pencil. Give each student a set of pipe cleaner pieces and a cotton ball. Invite students to make their own larva to glue to the larva section of their reproducible and glue the cotton ball to the underside of the branch in the pupa (chrysalis) section. Invite students to share their completed page with a partner.

Name_____ Date_____

The Growth of My Plant

Date	Plant "A" Height	Plant "B" Height	Comments

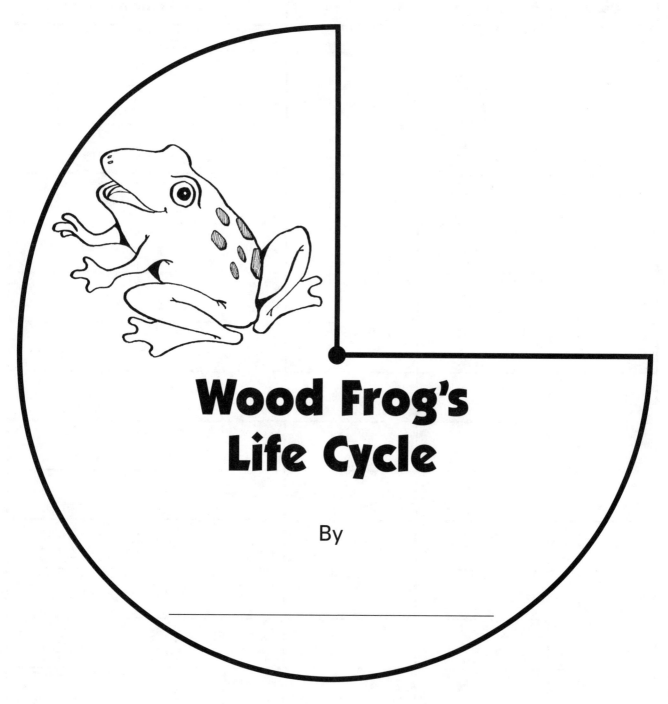

Wood Frog's Life Cycle

By

_____

Life Cycle Wheel, Part 2

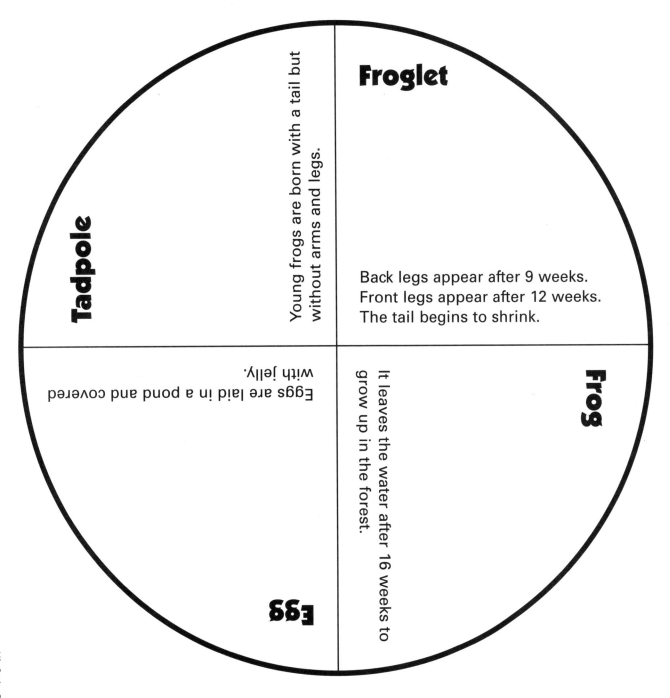

Froglet

Young frogs are born with a tail but without arms and legs.

Back legs appear after 9 weeks. Front legs appear after 12 weeks. The tail begins to shrink.

Tadpole

Eggs are laid in a pond and covered with jelly.

It leaves the water after 16 weeks to grow up in the forest.

Frog

Egg

Life Cycle Memory Cards

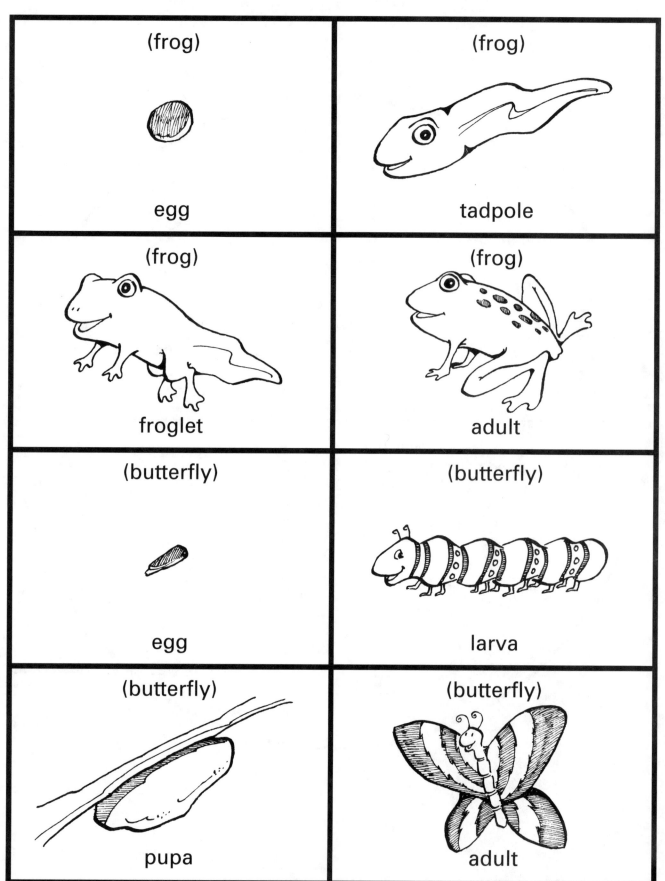

(frog)

egg

(frog)

tadpole

(frog)

froglet

(frog)

adult

(butterfly)

egg

(butterfly)

larva

(butterfly)

pupa

(butterfly)

adult

Life Cycle Memory Cards

(human)

baby

(human)

child

(human)

teenager

(human)

adult

(plant)

seed

(plant)

sprout

(plant)

plant

(plant)

mature plant drops seeds

Animal Life Cycle Cards

A _____ does not have any fur. It cannot see or hear at first.

After _____ emerges from an egg, it does not need its parents to care for it. It already knows how to swim and eat tiny plants and animals.

A newborn _____ is born live. It is the size of a bean when it crawls into its mother's pouch. It stays there for the next six months.

A newborn _____ is able to run and jump within a few hours of its birth. It is born live like a human.

Name_____ Date_____

Butterfly Life Cycle

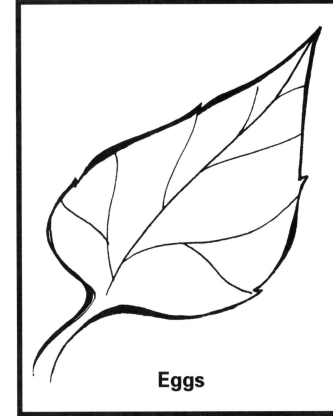

Eggs

Larva (caterpillar)

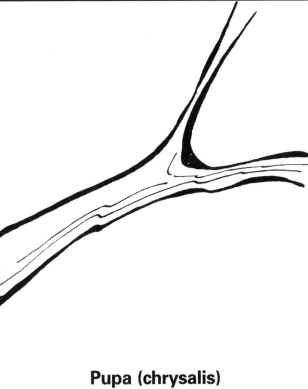

Pupa (chrysalis)

Adult Butterfly

Social Studies

Cycles of Life through History

OBJECTIVE

- Students will compare and contrast the lives of people long ago with people of today.

Discuss with students the four stages of the human life cycle (baby, child, teenager, adult). Ask students to describe each stage. Give each student a large sheet of construction paper. Have students fold it into thirds widthwise to make three columns. Ask them to turn their paper lengthwise and fold it in fifths to create three columns with five rows in each column. Have students leave the first row in the first column blank. Then, have them write *Baby* in the second row of the first column, *Child* in the third row, *Teenager* in the fourth row, and *Adult* in the fifth row. Ask students to write *Then* in the first row of the second column and *Now* in the first row of the third column. Have them work with a partner and use the recommended books to learn what it was like for a baby, a child, a teenager, and an adult to live in a previous period of time such as during the Civil War. Have students write a sentence or two about the experience in the appropriate boxes in the "Then" column. Ask them to consider what it is like for babies, children, teenagers, and adults to live now and write their ideas in the appropriate box in the "Now" column. Encourage pairs to share their work with each other.

If You Grew Up With Abraham Lincoln by Ann McGovern (Scholastic)

If You Lived 100 Years Ago by Ann McGovern (Scholastic)

If You Lived at the Time of the American Revolution by Kay Moore (Scholastic)

If You Lived at the Time of the Civil War by Kay Moore (Scholastic)

If You Lived at the Time of Martin Luther King by Ellen Levine (Scholastic)

If You Lived in Williamsburg in Colonial Days by Barbara Brenner (Scholastic)

Discussions Do Make a Difference

MATERIALS

● *The Great Kapok Tree: A Tale of the Amazon Rain Forest* by Lynn Cherry

● butcher paper

● crayons or markers

OBJECTIVE

● Students will discuss ways to help save our rain forests.

Read *The Great Kapok Tree* to the class, and discuss the importance of rain forests for the life cycle of both plants and animals. Write *native people, animals, trees and plants,* and *business people* in separate columns on the board. Tell students to imagine that they are a group of either native people, animals, business people, or trees and plants that live or work in a rain forest. Explain that the "business people" have come into the forest and cut down trees for lumber and gather plants to make medicines. Have students brainstorm five reasons each group is important to society. For example, students might say that the trees and plants provide us with medicine. Record student responses on the board. Hold a class discussion to determine what can be done to protect each group if the business people are allowed to use the resources of the rain forest. As a class, create a mural that shows the ways we can protect the rain forest.

Food from the Circle of Life

OBJECTIVES

Students will
● understand how a plant or an animal provides food for a society.
● brainstorm the role food production plays in our economy.

Draw a web with five "offshoots" on the top half of a piece of chart paper. Write the name of a plant or an animal with a life cycle the class has studied that is also a food source (e.g., chicken, cow, oat plant) in the center of the web. Prompt students to review the life cycle of this plant or animal, name some of the foods that are derived from it (e.g., ice cream, steak, cheese, milk), and write them in the offshoots of the web. Organize the class into five small groups, and assign each group one offshoot of the web. Give each group a piece of construction paper, and ask groups to draw their food. Display the pictures on a bulletin board titled *Life Cycles Give Us Food.* Discuss with students how the life cycle of the chosen plant or animal helps with the country's economy. To extend the activity, have students select a different food source and create a web for it.

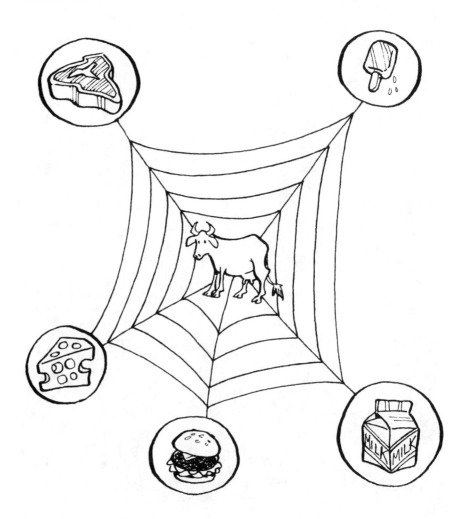

The Resources of a Region

OBJECTIVE

● Students will create a practical farm by making changes to current land.

MATERIALS

● Resources of a Region reproducible (page 60)

● crayons or markers

Ask students to brainstorm what resources a farmer might need to make a living. For example, students might say *land, shelter, water, animals,* and *electricity.* Record student responses on the board. Tell students that they will work with a partner to create a practical farm for a farmer to live on. Explain that they need to use the resources on their land to build a home and a barn and to establish their fields. Divide the class into pairs, and give each pair of students a Resources of a Region reproducible. Have students pretend to be farmers. Explain that parts of the environment on their land will need to be changed (e.g., clear a forest, dig irrigation ditches from the river, dig a pond) in order to create their farm. Tell students that the top portion of the reproducible shows what the land looks like presently. Ask students to create a farm by making changes to the current land and drawing their new farm in the box. Have partners asnwer the questions on the back of their paper. Invite partners to share with the class their changes to their farm (e.g., clear a forest), the reason for these changes (e.g., make room for a crop), and how the changes are helping or hurting the life cycle of the plants and animals on the farm.

- Life Cycles Business Report reproducible (page 61)
- reference materials and/or the Internet
- crayons or markers

Economically Speaking

OBJECTIVE

- Students will understand how industries depend on life cycles to earn money.

Explain to students that many people in various places of the world rely on a particular life cycle of a plant or an animal to help them earn the money they need to live. For example, there are a large number of dairy farmers in Wisconsin who raise the cows that provide milk for drinking or milk that is made into butter, cheese, or ice cream. These products are sold to other people all over the country. Brainstorm with students how other industries, such as fishing or farming, depend upon a life cycle to earn money. Record student responses on the board. Divide the class into small groups. Give each group a Life Cycles Business Report reproducible. Have group members write the name of an industry at the top of their paper, use reference materials and/or the Internet to research the life cycle related to their chosen business, and write a report that includes the type of climate needed. Have students draw a picture in the space provided. Invite groups to share their completed paper with the class.

Life Cycle Protection

OBJECTIVE

- Students will learn that the government plays a role in protecting endangered species.

Remind students that all living things have a life cycle. Ask students what endangered species are. Explain that the term *endangered species* refers to any living thing whose continued existence is threatened. Invite students to brainstorm animals that are in danger of extinction, such as blue whales, sea turtles, California condors, gray wolves, and steller sea lions. Record student responses on a piece of chart paper. Discuss with the class the possible reasons these animals are endangered (e.g., displacement due to human settlement or pollution caused by human industry). Tell students that the government often protects these animals by making laws. For example, people cannot go fishing without a license. People must pay a fine if they are caught touching a sea turtle. Ask students to name ways they can help protect the life cycle of the animals on their list. Invite students to work in small groups. Give each group two sentence strips and two construction paper squares. Have groups choose an animal from the list and write it on one sentence strip. Have them complete the frame *We can protect _____ by _____* on the second strip. Tell students to draw how the animals are in danger on the first construction paper square and how people can protect the animals on the second square. Give each group a hole punch and four pieces of string. Show students how to punch a hole at the top of each sentence strip and each construction paper square. Have groups punch a hole at the bottom center of the first sentence strip and two holes at the bottom of the second sentence strip. Then, have them use the string to connect the sentence strips and paper squares. Display the mobiles from the ceiling.

Resources of a Region

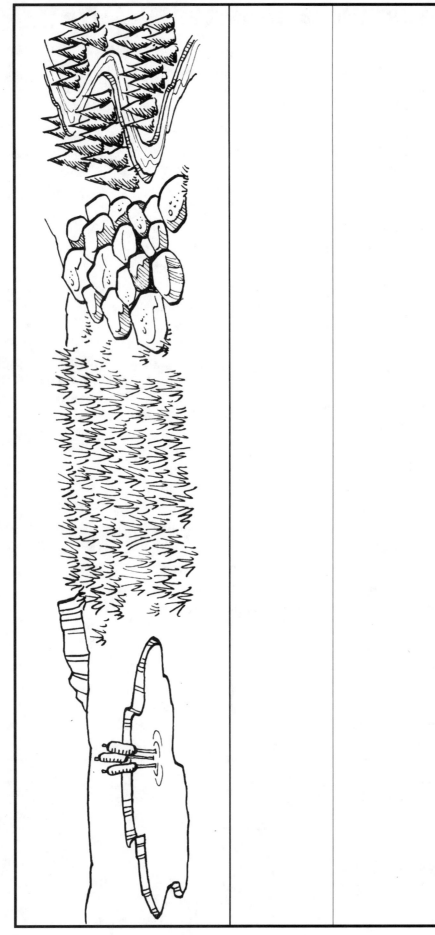

1 What changes did you make to the farm?

2 Why did you make these changes?

3 How are the changes helping the life cycle of the plants and animals on the farm?

4 How are the changes hurting the life cycle of the plants and animals on the farm?

Life Cycles Business Report

The _____ **Industry Is Doing Well!**

as reported by group members _____

_____

_____

_____

_____

_____

_____

Life Cycles Cumulative Test

Directions: Fill in the best answer for each question.

1 Which of the following is part of a life cycle?

(a) seed

(b) baby

(c) pupa

(d) all of the above

2 Which word would come **last** if the words were placed in alphabetical order?

(a) larva

(b) pupa

(c) adult

(d) egg

3 Circle the correct punctuation mark for the following sentence.

When will the egg hatch

(a) period (.)

(b) question mark (?)

(c) exclamation point (!)

(d) comma (,)

4 Which word **does not** rhyme with **sprout?**

(a) shout

(b) pout

(c) about

(d) loud

5 Which is the correct life cycle of a frog?

(a) egg, tadpole, froglet, frog

(b) frog, tadpole, egg, froglet

(c) egg, froglet, tadpole, frog

(d) egg, frog, froglet, tadpole

6 True or False: Every living thing has a life cycle.

(a) true

(b) false

Life Cycles © 2003 Creative Teaching Press

Name_____ Date_____

Life Cycles Cumulative Test

7 Which statement about life cycles is true?

   ⓐ Plants do not have life cycles.

   ⓑ Different groups of animals have different life cycles.

   ⓒ If an animal does not look like its parents when it was born, it never will.

   ⓓ A life cycle always begins with an egg.

8 Which sentence **does not** show alliteration?

   ⓐ The leaves of a lemon tree like light.

   ⓑ A spider's slippery silk saves it from getting stuck in its web.

   ⓒ A human baby cannot take care of itself.

   ⓓ A tadpole takes time to turn into a frog.

9 If you have six birds and they each lay five eggs, how many eggs are there altogether?

   ⓐ 22

   ⓑ 11

   ⓒ 30

   ⓓ 60

10 A snake lays twelve eggs. Four of the eggs have already hatched. How many more eggs still need to hatch?

   ⓐ 16

   ⓑ 8

   ⓒ 12

   ⓓ 4

11 Describe the stages of the life cycle of a bee, a plant, or a caterpillar.

_____

_____

12 Why do you think some animals leave their mother right after birth and other animals stay with their mother for a longer period of time?

_____

_____

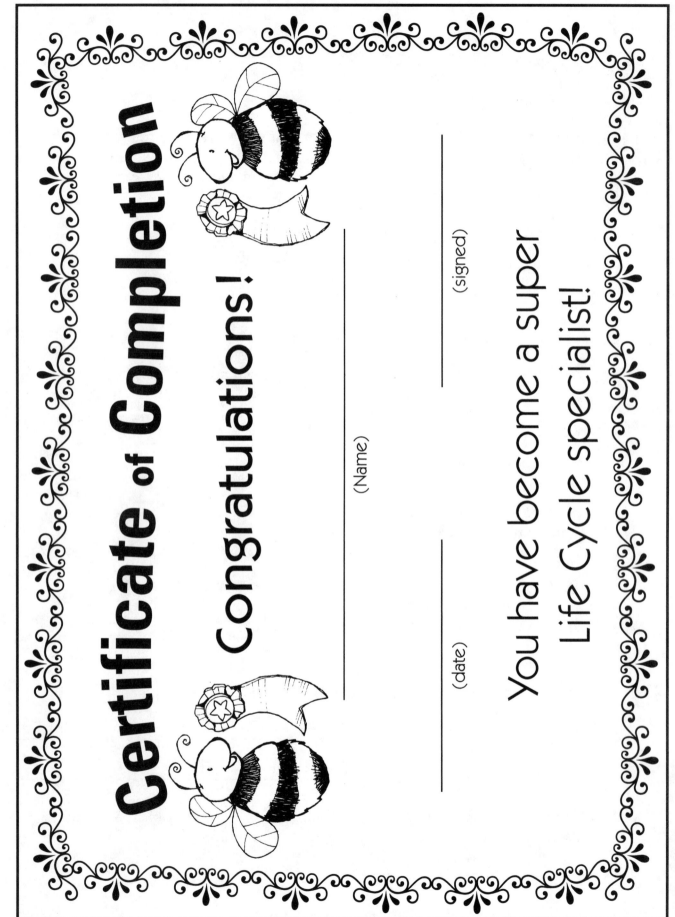

Certificate of Completion

Congratulations!

_____
(Name)

_____
(date)

_____
(signed)

You have become a super
Life Cycle specialist!